MY FIRST BOOK OF
ELECTROMAGNETISM

DISCOVERING THE WORLD OF ELECTRICITY

**EDUARD ALTARRIBA &
SHEDDAD KAID-SALAH FERRÓN**

Button
BOOKS

CONTENTS

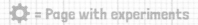 ⚙ = Page with experiments

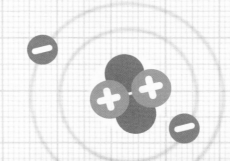

INTRODUCTION

You go into your room. Everything's dark. You feel your way along the wall to find the light switch. Easy. You know where it is. The instant you push it, the room lights up, as if by magic.

Nowadays, electricity and magnetism are all around us and we use them for nearly everything. In fact, it's hard to imagine a world without them.

We use electricity and magnetism to light our houses and our streets, keep our fridges cold, cook food with microwaves, heat the water for our showers, watch TV, play video games, surf the internet on our computers, send messages on our phones, listen to music with earphones . . . the list is endless.

But, what actually is ELECTRICITY? What has it got to do with magnets? What is MAGNETISM? And the most fascinating thing of all, what has all this got to do with LIGHT?

We will answer these and other questions in this book as we venture into the fabulous world of ELECTROMAGNETISM.

WELCOME TO THIS AMAZING JOURNEY!

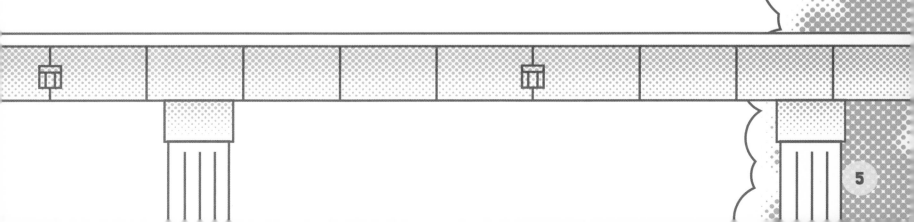

Around 4,800 years ago, the ancient Egyptians were already writing about electric catfish, which could produce electric shocks to defend themselves. They were called "Thunder of the Nile."

ELECTRICAL PHENOMENA

Humans have always been aware of the effects of electricity, even before we knew what it was or where it came from.

Ancient civilizations knew about the effects of electricity in the atmosphere, in particular LIGHTNING. They used mythology to explain this extraordinary natural phenomenon.

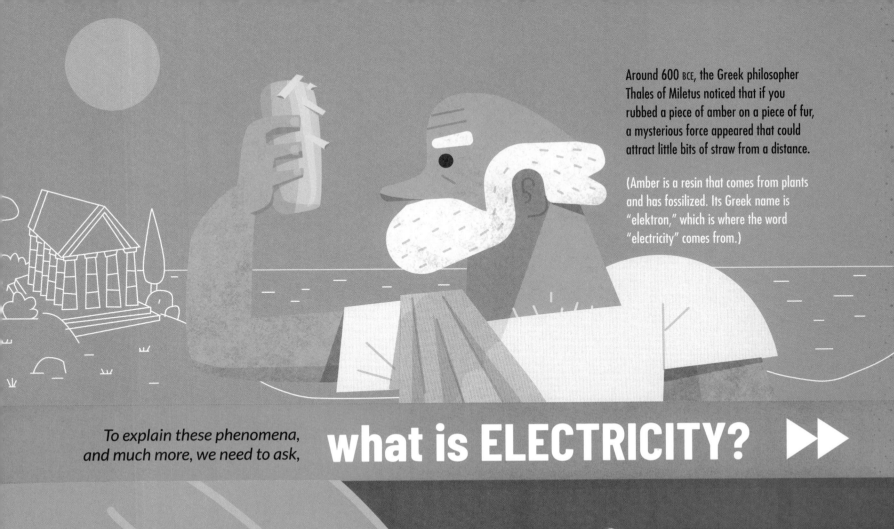

Around 600 BCE, the Greek philosopher Thales of Miletus noticed that if you rubbed a piece of amber on a piece of fur, a mysterious force appeared that could attract little bits of straw from a distance.

(Amber is a resin that comes from plants and has fossilized. Its Greek name is "elektron," which is where the word "electricity" comes from.)

To explain these phenomena, and much more, we need to ask, **what is ELECTRICITY?** ▶▶

In the same way, when we run a plastic comb through our hair, the same mysterious "electrical" force appears, causing the hair to be attracted to the plastic.

ELECTRIC CHARGE

ELECTRIC CHARGE is a property of matter (the stuff things are made of) that explains all the electrical phenomena we see.

A BODY CAN HAVE AN ELECTRIC CHARGE

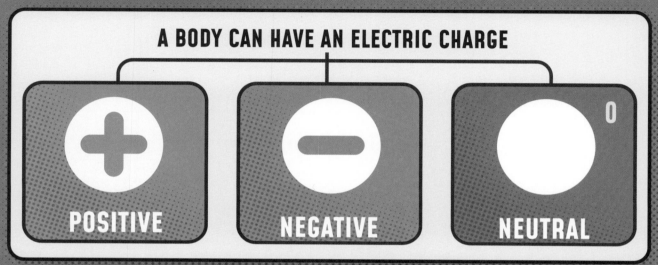

POSITIVE   **NEGATIVE**   **NEUTRAL** (0)

FRANKLIN'S PORTRAIT IS PRINTED ON $100 BILLS.

The first person to come up with the idea of electric charge, thanks to a series of experiments he did, was the American scientist **BENJAMIN FRANKLIN** (1706–1790).

We're going to reproduce these experiments using two glass rods, two amber (or plastic) rods, and a silk handkerchief.

 If we put two of the rods together, nothing happens, no force passes between them. But we're going to see what happens if we rub the different rods on the silk handkerchief.

When we rub a glass rod on the silk, we see that if we move the hankie and the rod toward each other, a force attracts them to each another.

If we rub an amber rod on the silk, when we move them together, they are also attracted to each another.

If we rub two glass rods on the silk, a force appears that pushes them apart: they repel each another.

The same happens with two amber rods rubbed on the silk: they repel each another as well.

However, when you take a glass rod and an amber rod that have been rubbed on the silk and move them closer to each another, a force attracts them.

Thanks to these experiments, Franklin worked out that:

Matter has a physical property—an electric charge—which explains electrical phenomena.

The charge has to come from *neutral objects*, because there is no charge at first and it only appears when we rub them.

There are two types of charges with different signs:

POSITIVE ➕ **and** NEGATIVE ➖

Electric charges exert a force on other electric charges in such a way that:

If the charges are a different sign,
THEY ARE ATTRACTED

➕ →•← ➖

If the charges are the same sign,
THEY ARE REPELLED

➕ → ➕ | ➖ ←→ ➖

But, where does the charge come from if neither the glass nor the amber nor the silk are charged before you rub them?

PARTICLES AND CHARGE

Almost all known matter is made up of **ATOMS.**

ATOMS are tiny particles that, in turn, are formed of even smaller particles: protons, neutrons, and electrons.

They are like the building blocks that everything is made of: your hair, the planet Mars, the tip of your nose, and the air you breathe.

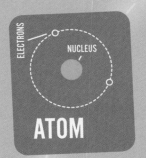

ELECTRONS

NUCLEUS

ATOM

PROTONS and **NEUTRONS** have a similar mass and are found in the **NUCLEUS** of the atom.

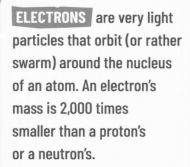

ELECTRONS are very light particles that orbit (or rather swarm) around the nucleus of an atom. An electron's mass is 2,000 times smaller than a proton's or a neutron's.

An atom is really tiny. To give you an idea: there are around 5,000,000,000,000,000,000,000 atoms in a drop of water.

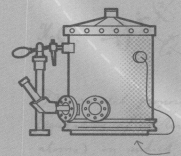

The American physicist Robert A. Millikan (1868–1953) was the first to perform an experiment to measure an electron's charge.

And he did it with a machine like this!

As we've said, electric charge is an essential property of matter. Some particles have charge, some don't.

But, watch out, we can't add charge to a particle or remove charge from it. Each particle is how it is.

Protons
have positive electric charge.

ELECTRONS AND PROTONS HAVE THE SAME ELECTRIC CHARGE BUT THE OPPOSITE SIGN.

So, they attract.

Neutrons
don't have electric charge.
They are **NEUTRAL**, hence their name.

 NUCLEUS

Electrons
have negative electric charge.

e

The electric charge of electrons and protons is the smallest of all. It is called an ELEMENTARY CHARGE and its symbol is the letter "e."

When an object is electrically charged, its total charge ("q") is the sum of lots of elementary charges. For example, a charge of 2 electrons would be $q = -2e$, while a charge of a million protons would be $q = 1,000,000e$

IONIZATION

When an atom has the same number of electrons and protons, its electric charge is zero and it is NEUTRAL.

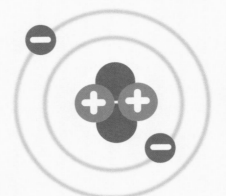

When this balance is disturbed, IONIZATION occurs.

When an atom gains or loses electrons, it becomes an ION.

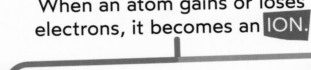

There are MORE electrons than protons.

An atom with excess electrons is NEGATIVELY charged

(it's a negative ion).

There are FEWER electrons than protons.

An atom that has lost electrons is POSITIVELY charged

(it's a positive ion).

Now we know that charges come from atoms, we can understand our experiments better.

When we rub a glass rod on a silk handkerchief, we move some electrons from the glass onto the silk.

Both materials are now charged. The glass rod has lost electrons and is now positively charged +q while the silk handkerchief has more electrons (the ones it has taken from the glass) and is negatively charged -q .

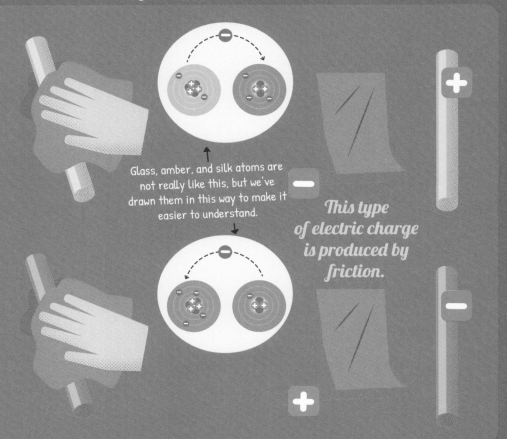

Glass, amber, and silk atoms are not really like this, but we've drawn them in this way to make it easier to understand.

This type of electric charge is produced by friction.

Whereas, when we rub the amber rod on the silk handkerchief, exactly the opposite happens and this time the silk transfers electrons on to the amber, so the silk is positively charged +q and the amber negatively charged -q .

CONDUCTORS and INSULATORS

There are materials, like metals, for example, in which some of the electrons can move freely. These materials are called CONDUCTORS.

Whereas, there are other materials like wood or plastic in which all the electrons are bound to their atoms and cannot move freely. We call these materials INSULATORS.

Not all electrons can move freely in materials.

CHARGE IS CONSERVED!

As we have seen, atoms have the same number of electrons and protons, which makes their electric charge zero: **THEY ARE NEUTRAL.**

If you take an object (for example, our glass rod) and remove 10 electrons, it will then be positively charged with a charge of q = +10e.

Where have these 10 electrons that we've removed from the glass gone? Well, they've stayed in the silk handkerchief, which is now negatively charged with a charge of q = –10e.

total q = glass q + silk q = +10e – 10e = 0

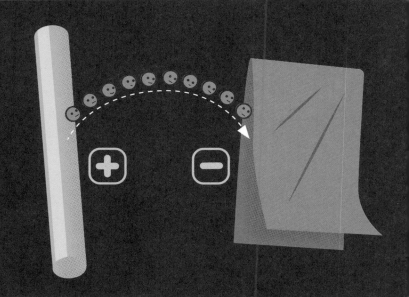

Law of conservation of charge

In a process of ionization, the total number of electrons and protons does not change, the only thing we do is separate them.

Charge doesn't come from thin air, nor does it just disappear. Or, to put it another way, **electric charge is neither created nor destroyed.**

Thanks to his experiments, Benjamin Franklin realized that charge is conserved.

Objects tend to be neutral. When we rub two objects together we transfer electricity from one to the other and both are equally charged, one positively and the other negatively.

This principle or law is one of the few conservation laws in the Universe.

Thor, the God of Thunder, adding and subtracting electric charges

The world is neutral, electrically speaking: it has the same number of positive charges and negative charges. If someone added up all the positive charges and subtracted all the negative charges, the result would be zero.

15

ELECTROSCOPES

These are instruments used to measure the presence of electric charge in an object.

Ball of conductive material insulated from the rest of the device to stop electric charges from escaping

Stem of conductive material

Cap made of nonconductive material that insulates the device

Container

Two conductive leaves that are together when there is no electric charge

Charging by friction

Negatively charged plastic rod (we can also use a balloon).

We rub the rod beforehand on a woolen cloth to charge it (wool works better than silk).

If we touch the ball with an object that has an electric charge, someof the charge in the object will transfer to the electroscope.

The ball and the metal leaves become charged.

The leaves separate because charges of the same sign repel.

When we remove the charged object, the electroscope stays charged, but if we touch the ball with a neutral object, the electroscope will lose all the charge and become neutral again (the sheets come back together).

Charging by induction

If we bring the negatively charged plastic rod close to the ball, the two leaves also separate.

The charges have been created by induction. The rod has not touched the ball, so we haven't transferred any electric charge to the electroscope.

This happens because, when you bring the rod close, the free electrons in the conductive materials are repelled by the negative charge and start moving.

The ball loses electrons and becomes positively charged. The leaves gain those electrons to become negatively charged, and repel each other.

When we move the rod away, the electrons spread out around the conductive materials again, and the sheets move together.

HOMEMADE ELECTROSCOPE

We can make our own electroscope.

We will need:

A glass jar (such as a pickling jar)	Polystyrene	Tin foil	Copper wire (you can use an insulated electric wire with the ends stripped off)

1 Draw around the rim of the jar on the polystyrene, then cut out the circle using a craft knife (ask an adult to help you with the cutting).

 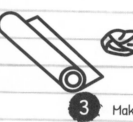

2 Cut two tin foil leaves.

3 Make a ball of tin foil.

4 Push the copper wire through the polystyrene.

5 Hang the two tin foil leaves from one end of the wire.

6 Place the tin foil ball on the top part of the wire.

7 Fit the polystyrene into the glass jar. Make sure it's a tight fit—you may need to push it so it squeezes in.

And that's our electroscope ready!

EXPERIMENTS WITH BALLOONS

WE'RE GOING TO PLAY A BIT WITH ELECTRICITY.

To do all the experiments, first you have to rub an inflated balloon on your hair so that it acquires electrons (which it takes from your hair) and becomes negatively charged.

Hair sticking out

If you put the charged balloon near someone's head, you'll see their hair lift up and separate.

Paper hunt

Put some pieces of paper on a table. If you put the charged balloon near them, you'll see how they are attracted.

Testing our homemade electroscope

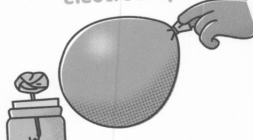

Put the charged balloon near the tin foil ball and you'll see how the foil leaves separate. If you touch the ball with the balloon and then move it away, the leaves will stay separated because the electroscope has stayed charged.

ELECTRIC FORCE BETWEEN TWO CHARGES

Charles-Augustin de Coulomb (1736-1806) was a French physicist and mathematician who studied electricity.

Coulomb discovered that there is an "electric" force between two charges, which is applied by one charge on the other along the straight line joining them.

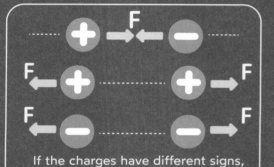

If the charges have different signs, the force is attractive (it attracts), and if they have the same sign, the force is repulsive (it repels).

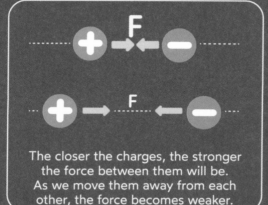

The closer the charges, the stronger the force between them will be. As we move them away from each other, the force becomes weaker.

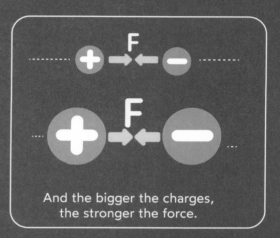

And the bigger the charges, the stronger the force.

FIELD OF AN ELECTRIC CHARGE

The idea that electric force works at a distance is quite mind-boggling. To explain why electric force does not need the charges to be in contact, it's helpful to imagine that there is an area of space around an electric charge. If we put another charge into that space, it will apply a force on the first charge without the two charges touching each another.

This area of space is an ELECTRIC FIELD and the symbol used for it is the capital letter E.

We can show an electric field using "lines of force" or "field lines."

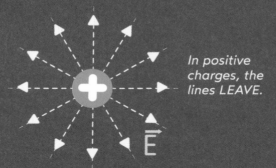

In positive charges, the lines LEAVE.

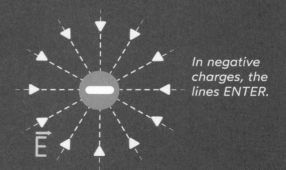

In negative charges, the lines ENTER.

ELECTRIC CURRENT

Electric current is produced when electric charges move around inside a material.

MOVE!

Charges are usually free electrons in a conductor. To get them to move, something has to push or attract them.

As we have seen, charges with a different sign **attract**, and charges with the same sign **repel**.

If we want to move electrons inside a metal cable, copper for example, what we would do is put positive electric charges on one end and negative electric charges on the other.

In this way, electrons (which have a negative charge) would be attracted by positive charges and pushed by negative charges, and so would move around inside the cable. Then we would have **ELECTRIC CURRENT**.

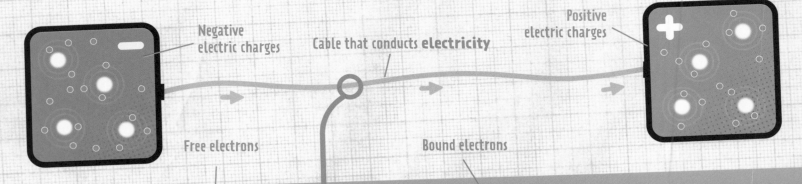

Negative electric charges

Cable that conducts **electricity**

Positive electric charges

Free electrons

Bound electrons

ELECTRIC CIRCUIT

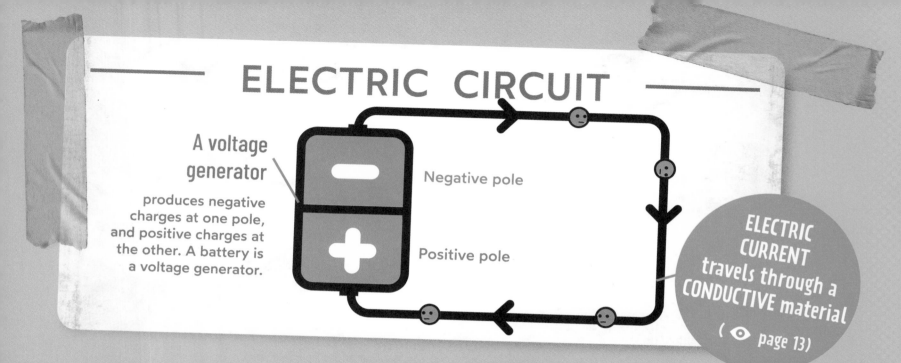

A voltage generator produces negative charges at one pole, and positive charges at the other. A battery is a voltage generator.

Negative pole

Positive pole

ELECTRIC CURRENT travels through a CONDUCTIVE material (👁 page 13)

VOLTAGE (or potential difference)

Voltage creates current.

The more positive and negative charges we put on the poles of an electric circuit, the faster the electrons will move around inside the circuit, as they will be attracted by the positive pole and repelled by the negative one with more force. This means the electric current will be greater.

A PLUG SOCKET IS HIGH VOLTAGE AND PRODUCES CURRENT. DON'T EVEN THINK ABOUT PUTTING YOUR FINGERS IN ONE!!

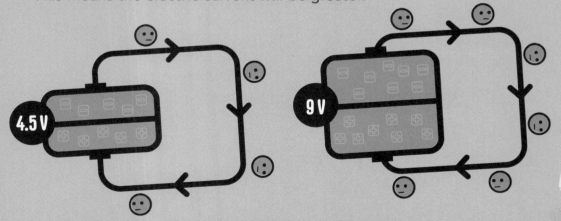

4.5 V

9 V

VOLTAGE or POTENTIAL DIFFERENCE is due to the difference between the amount of positive and negative charges (the "potential") at the two poles. This determines the energy that the electrons will gain.

Batteries

There are lots of different types and sizes of batteries, and they are everywhere, from phones to car batteries. We use them to obtain electrical energy.

An electric battery is a device for storing chemical energy and converting it into electric current.

In an ELECTROCHEMICAL CELL, chemical reactions are used to obtain electrical energy.

To make an electrochemical cell we need two chemical elements, for example copper (Cu) and zinc (Zn), and a liquid that conducts electricity called an electrolyte, which in our case will be water with salt.

When you connect the two metal plates, the zinc (Zn) atoms lose electrons, which travel across the cable to the copper (Cu) atoms.

The electric charges carry on moving across the electrolyte, which gives us a closed electric circuit.

This movement of electrons between the two metals creates an ELECTRIC CURRENT.

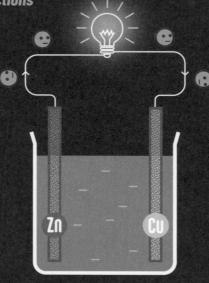

Some batteries are made of lots of electrochemical cells put together.

Other batteries are made of a single electrochemical cell that is slightly more sophisticated.

MAKING A HOMEMADE BATTERY

In 1800, Alessandro Volta presented to the world the VOLTAIC PILE, the first electric battery. It was created by piling copper and zinc plates on top of one another, separated by pieces of cardboard soaked in salt water. When the two poles of the pile, or battery, were connected, an electric current was produced.

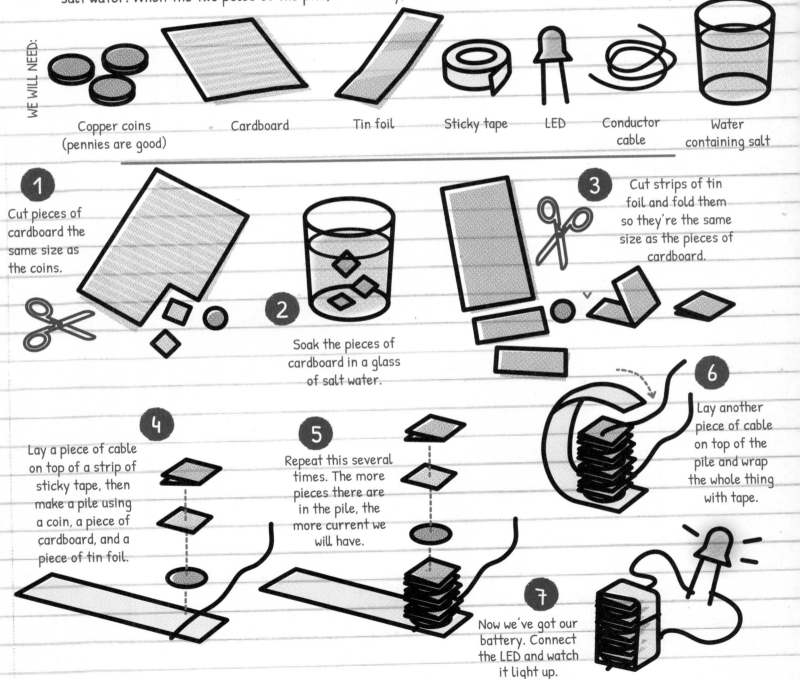

WE WILL NEED:

Copper coins (pennies are good)

Cardboard

Tin foil

Sticky tape

LED

Conductor cable

Water containing salt

1 Cut pieces of cardboard the same size as the coins.

2 Soak the pieces of cardboard in a glass of salt water.

3 Cut strips of tin foil and fold them so they're the same size as the pieces of cardboard.

4 Lay a piece of cable on top of a strip of sticky tape, then make a pile using a coin, a piece of cardboard, and a piece of tin foil.

5 Repeat this several times. The more pieces there are in the pile, the more current we will have.

6 Lay another piece of cable on top of the pile and wrap the whole thing with tape.

7 Now we've got our battery. Connect the LED and watch it light up.

Magnetism

Magnetism is a natural phenomenon that makes certain materials attract or repel.

You must have played with a MAGNET before.

A magnet is an object that can attract metals like iron or other magnets from a "distance."

Natural magnets

As far back as 800 BCE in ancient Greece, in the Magnesia region (which is where we get the word "magnetism"), it was known that some rocks attracted iron. They were called MAGNETIC stones and they were made of magnetite, a mineral with magnetic properties commonly found in that area.

The Greek philosopher Thales of Miletus (624–546 BCE) studied electricity (👁 page 7) as well as the phenomenon of magnetism.

MAGNETS

A magnet has a NORTH pole and a SOUTH pole.

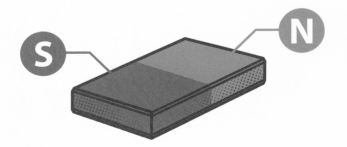

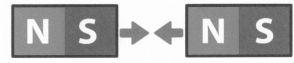

The closer two magnets are, the greater the force between them.

When we put the same poles—either north or south—of two magnets close to each other, they exert a repulsive force and repel each other. Whereas, if we put the opposite poles of the magnets together, we see that the force attracts one to the other.

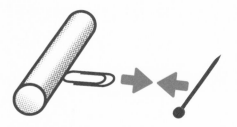

If we put a magnet close to a piece of iron, it doesn't matter which pole we present, the piece of iron and the magnet are attracted.

The piece of iron has been affected by the magnet and has temporarily become a magnet itself, with its own north and south poles. It would also be able to attract other pieces of iron.

As we've already seen, particles with charge only have a single type of charge: either positive or negative.

Magnets, however, can't have a single type of pole. They always have two poles, north and south.

Thanks to this property, a strange thing happens with magnets: if we split a magnet in two pieces, we get two magnets, each with north and south poles.

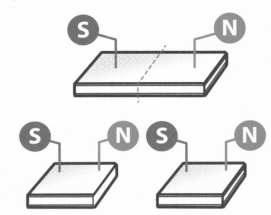

THE MAGNETIC FIELD OF A MAGNET

 ## EXPERIMENT WITH IRON FILINGS

Iron filings are tiny pieces of iron.

▶ Put a pile of iron filings on a sheet of paper. They don't have to be tidy.

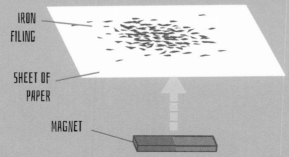

IRON FILING

SHEET OF PAPER

MAGNET

▶ If we put a magnet under the piece of paper, something very strange happens.

▶ When the magnet is there, the filings tidy themselves up and arrange themselves in a pattern, as we can see in this drawing.

S

The filings show us the LINES OF FORCE of the magnet's MAGNETIC FIELD.

This pattern gives us an idea of the force that is acting on the filings.

In the parts where the lines of force (page 19) are closer together, the magnetic field is stronger. Where they are more spaced out, it is weaker.

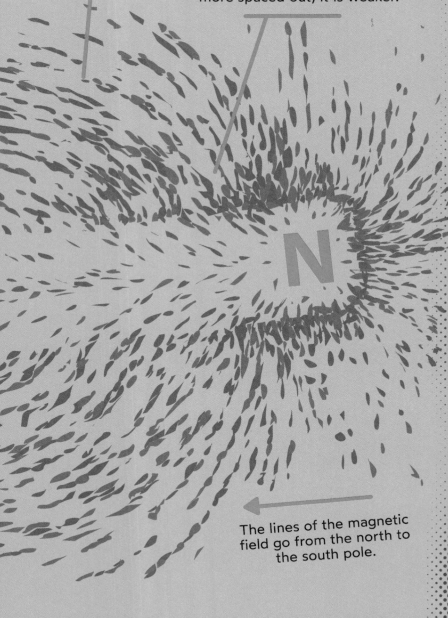

The lines of the magnetic field go from the north to the south pole.

The lines of force or field lines are generated by the magnet and, although they are invisible, they are always there. Only the iron filings show us where the field lines are.

The space where the magnets exert their influence on other magnets or on moving charges (represented by the field lines) is the

MAGNETIC FIELD

and the symbol we use for it is the capital letter B.

The Earth is a giant magnet

The Earth's interior behaves like a magnet that generates the Earth's magnetic field (called the geomagnetic field).

Like all magnets, it has a north and a south pole, and its axis is close to the Earth's axis of rotation.

This field is generated by the Earth's outer core, a mass of molten iron and nickel. As this mass of liquid metal moves, it creates electric currents that produce the magnetic field (◉ page 30).

COMPASSES

A compass needle is a magnet that, like all magnets, orients itself when it is in a magnetic field. The Earth's geomagnetic field causes the magnetic needle of a compass to always point in the same direction: the Earth's magnetic north pole.

The compass always points to the magnetic north and that is why we use it to get our bearings.

Apparently, Chinese sailors were the first to use a compass to navigate.

In actual fact, we can use a compass to detect any magnetic field, not just the Earth's one. If you move a compass toward a magnet you'll see that it goes a bit crazy, as it will orient itself according to the poles of the magnet. Try it with a fridge magnet, or a phone or a tablet (these both contain magnets).

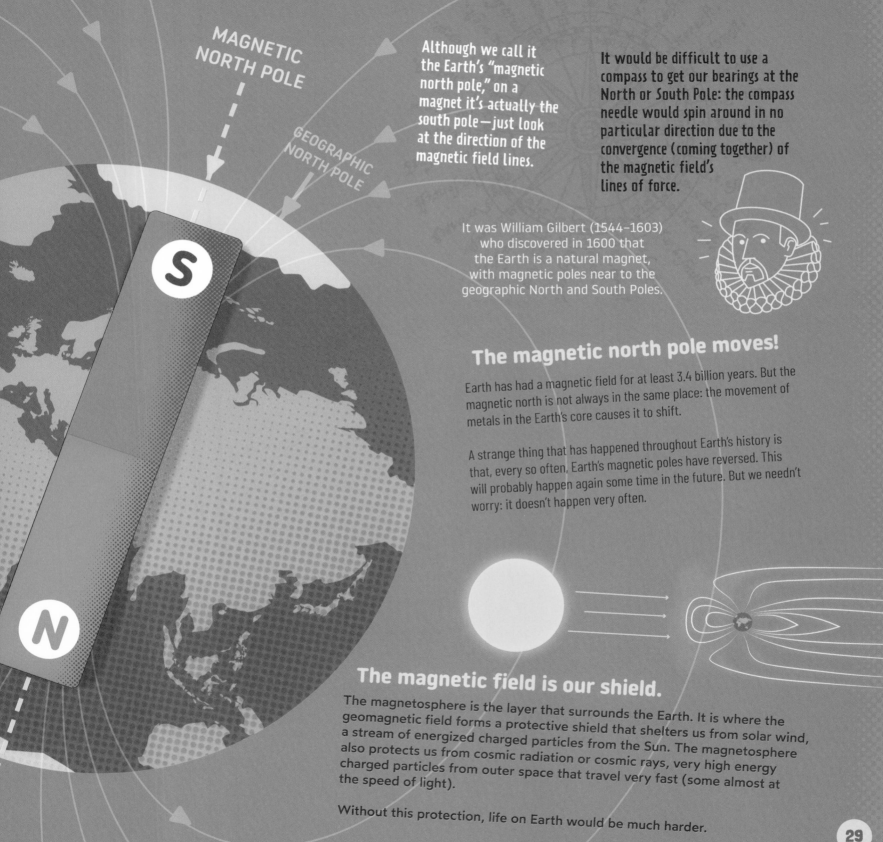

MAGNETIC NORTH POLE

GEOGRAPHIC NORTH POLE

S

N

Although we call it the Earth's "magnetic north pole," on a magnet it's actually the south pole—just look at the direction of the magnetic field lines.

It would be difficult to use a compass to get our bearings at the North or South Pole: the compass needle would spin around in no particular direction due to the convergence (coming together) of the magnetic field's lines of force.

It was William Gilbert (1544–1603) who discovered in 1600 that the Earth is a natural magnet, with magnetic poles near to the geographic North and South Poles.

The magnetic north pole moves!

Earth has had a magnetic field for at least 3.4 billion years. But the magnetic north is not always in the same place: the movement of metals in the Earth's core causes it to shift.

A strange thing that has happened throughout Earth's history is that, every so often, Earth's magnetic poles have reversed. This will probably happen again some time in the future. But we needn't worry: it doesn't happen very often.

The magnetic field is our shield.

The magnetosphere is the layer that surrounds the Earth. It is where the geomagnetic field forms a protective shield that shelters us from solar wind, a stream of energized charged particles from the Sun. The magnetosphere also protects us from cosmic radiation or cosmic rays, very high energy charged particles from outer space that travel very fast (some almost at the speed of light).

Without this protection, life on Earth would be much harder.

Electricity generates magnetism

Hans Christian Ørsted (1777–1851) was a Danish physicist and chemist who discovered, while doing experiments, that there was a connection between electricity and magnetism.

In 1820, he did an experiment that was to prove crucial to physics.

Ørsted placed a compass near a conductor wire connected to a battery.

When he passed an electric current through the conductor wire, he saw that the compass's **magnetic needle changed direction so that it was at right angles to the wire** through which the current was passing.

So this experiment showed that passing an electric current through a conductor generates a magnetic field.

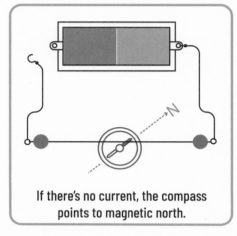

If there's no current, the compass points to magnetic north.

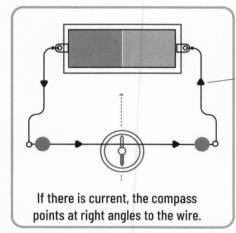

Direction of movement of electrons

If there is current, the compass points at right angles to the wire.

Ørsted's experiment had shown there was a connection between electricity and magnetism.

Bear in mind that back then, people believed that electricity and magnetism were two different phenomenon and were totally unrelated to one another.

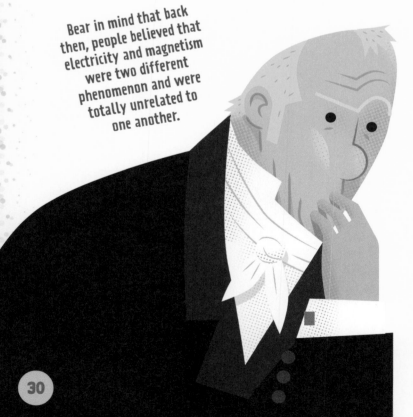

ELECTROMAGNETISM WAS BORN!

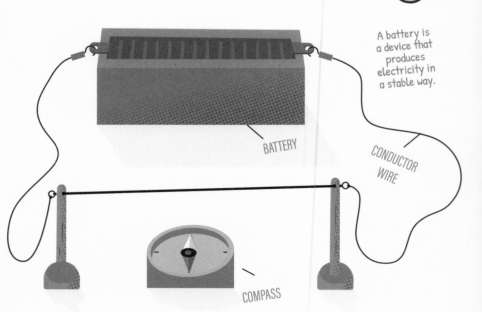

A battery is a device that produces electricity in a stable way.

BATTERY

CONDUCTOR WIRE

COMPASS

André-Marie Ampère (1775–1836) was a French physicist and mathematician. When he found out about Ørsted's work, he became extremely interested in the relationship between electricity and magnetism and he started researching it.

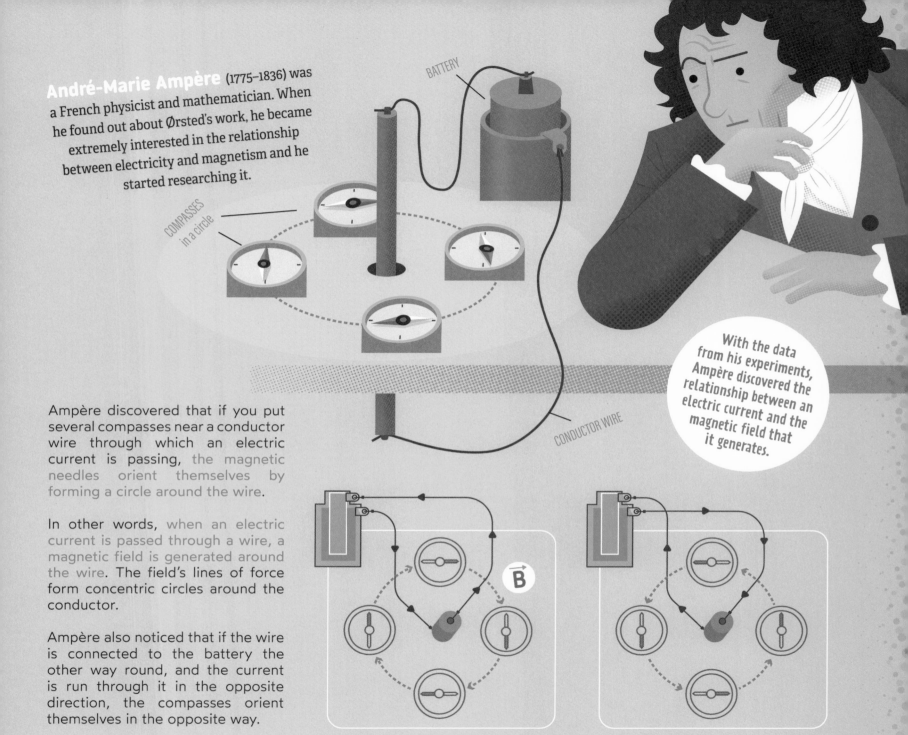

BATTERY

COMPASSES in a circle

CONDUCTOR WIRE

With the data from his experiments, Ampère discovered the relationship between an electric current and the magnetic field that it generates.

Ampère discovered that if you put several compasses near a conductor wire through which an electric current is passing, the magnetic needles orient themselves by forming a circle around the wire.

In other words, when an electric current is passed through a wire, a magnetic field is generated around the wire. The field's lines of force form concentric circles around the conductor.

Ampère also noticed that if the wire is connected to the battery the other way round, and the current is run through it in the opposite direction, the compasses orient themselves in the opposite way.

$\vec{B}$

Bear in mind that an electric current is nothing more than moving electric charges, so we can conclude that:

A moving electric charge generates a magnetic field.

Electromagnets

Now we know that we can generate magnetic fields with electricity, it makes sense that an electromagnet is a magnet generated by an electric current.

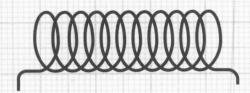

A solenoid is a coil of conductor wire rolled into a shape with several spirals together, like a spring.

What happens if we run an electric current through a solenoid?
Well, we create a magnetic field similar to the one around a natural magnet.

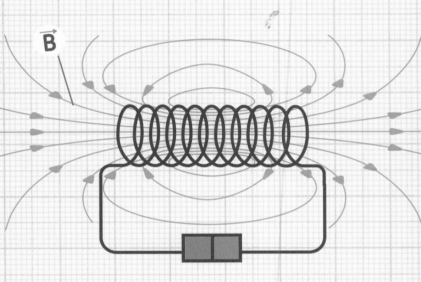

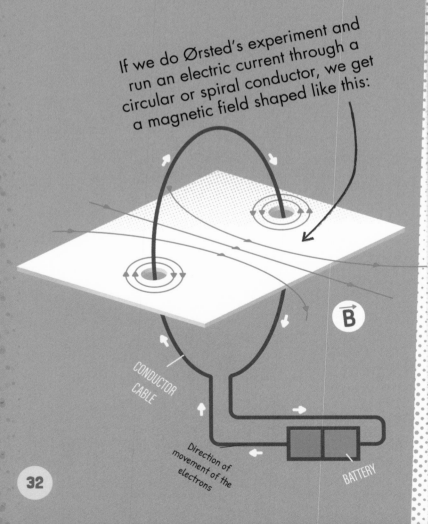

If we do Ørsted's experiment and run an electric current through a circular or spiral conductor, we get a magnetic field shaped like this:

B⃗

CONDUCTOR CABLE

Direction of movement of the electrons

BATTERY

So what we have is an ELECTROMAGNET.

The larger the current, the stronger the force of the magnetic field generated by the electromagnet.

And, of course, if we turn off the current, we won't have a magnetic field any more.

If we put an iron rod inside the coil used to make the solenoid, and we run the current through it, the iron becomes magnetic and this creates an even bigger magnetic field.

$\vec{B}$

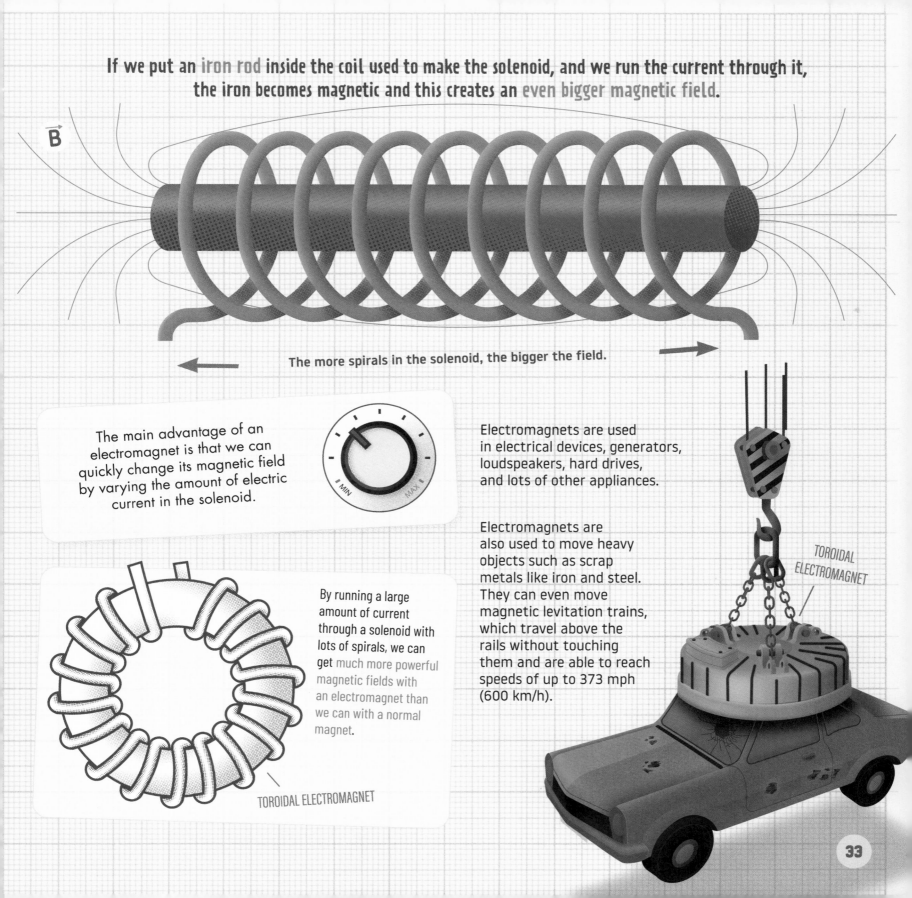

The more spirals in the solenoid, the bigger the field.

The main advantage of an electromagnet is that we can quickly change its magnetic field by varying the amount of electric current in the solenoid.

MIN   MAX

By running a large amount of current through a solenoid with lots of spirals, we can get much more powerful magnetic fields with an electromagnet than we can with a normal magnet.

TOROIDAL ELECTROMAGNET

Electromagnets are used in electrical devices, generators, loudspeakers, hard drives, and lots of other appliances.

Electromagnets are also used to move heavy objects such as scrap metals like iron and steel. They can even move magnetic levitation trains, which travel above the rails without touching them and are able to reach speeds of up to 373 mph (600 km/h).

TOROIDAL ELECTROMAGNET

Electric motors

We find electric motors in lots of machines, tools, and home appliances that we use every day.

An electric motor is a machine that converts electricity into rotating motion.

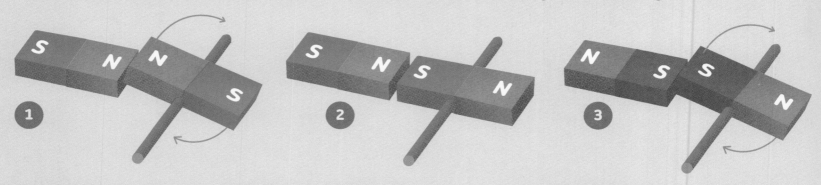

As we've just seen, if we apply an electric current to a solenoid, we generate a magnetic field and get an ELECTROMAGNET.

If we mount an electromagnet on an axle and place an electromagnet with the same polarity next to it (1), the same poles repel one another and the electromagnet will start to rotate until the opposite poles are lined up (2).

And if we change the polarity of the electromagnet beside it (3), the poles will be the same, so they will repel each another and the electromagnetic will start rotating again.

AND SO WE HAVE MOVEMENT.

COILS

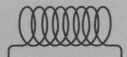 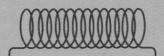 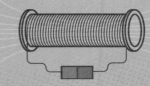

The more spirals a solenoid has, the greater the magnetic field it will generate as an electromagnet.

A solenoid is a type of **COIL**. A coil has lots of spirals very close together. It usually consists of a conductor cable or wire wound around a core, which can either

be hollow or made of a ferromagnetic material like iron to make it stronger. Electromagnets in electric motors are usually coils.

Making a homemade ELECTRIC MOTOR

Two safety pins   Thin copper wire   D-cell 1.5 volt battery   Sticky tape   Magnet

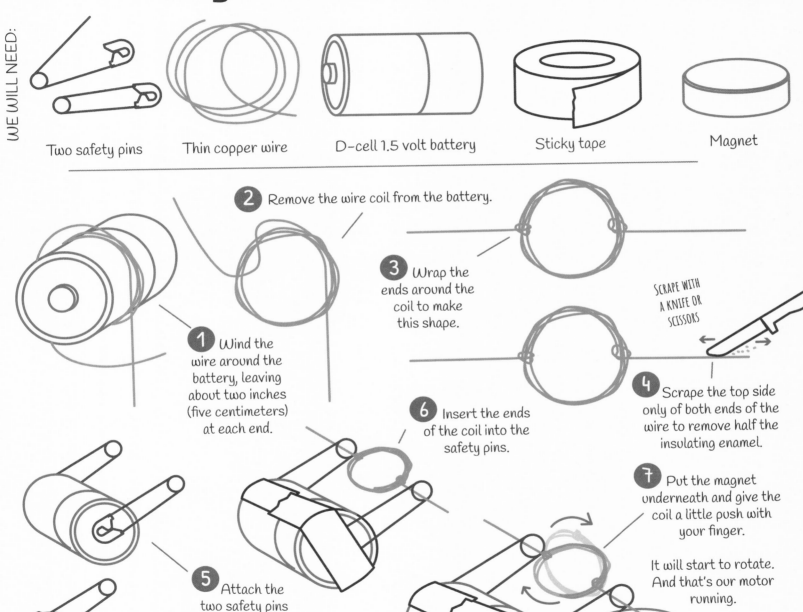

2 Remove the wire coil from the battery.

3 Wrap the ends around the coil to make this shape.

1 Wind the wire around the battery, leaving about two inches (five centimeters) at each end.

SCRAPE WITH A KNIFE OR SCISSORS

4 Scrape the top side only of both ends of the wire to remove half the insulating enamel.

6 Insert the ends of the coil into the safety pins.

5 Attach the two safety pins to the ends of the battery using sticky tape.

7 Put the magnet underneath and give the coil a little push with your finger.

It will start to rotate. And that's our motor running.

35

Why are some materials magnetic?

The electric charges (basically the electrons) in an atom turn as much around themselves as they do around the nucleus. These movements create tiny electric currents that, in turn, produce magnetic microfields.

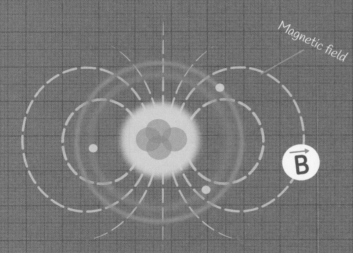

Magnetic field

$\vec{B}$

Because of this an atom can behave like a

MINI-MAGNET.

André-Marie Ampère (1775–1836) was the first person to suggest that magnets had microscopic currents.

As we've already seen, if we split a magnet into two parts, both fragments have two magnetic poles, north and south; we get two magnets. If we continue splitting the fragments, we'll get smaller and weaker magnets.

But how far can we carry on splitting magnets? If we carry on splitting the fragments of the magnet until we get tiny particles of material, we can deduce that the atoms of the magnet would behave like mini-magnets.

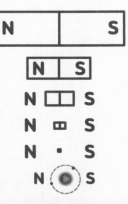

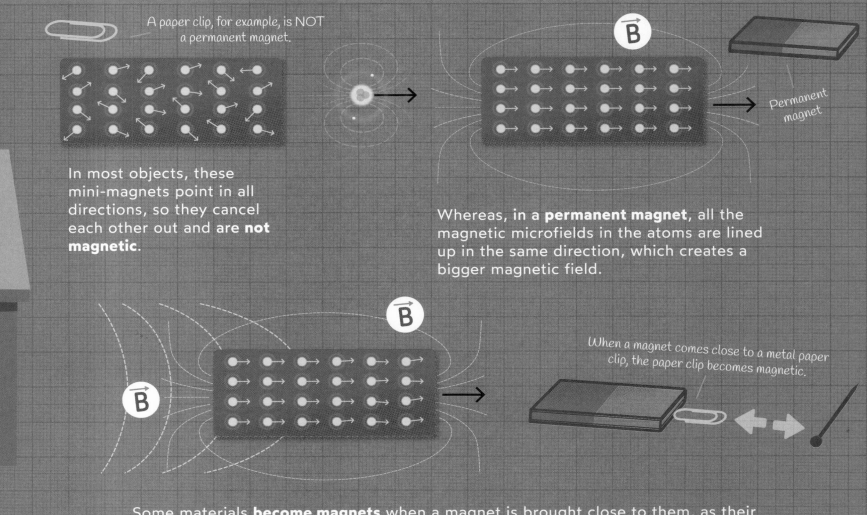

A paper clip, for example, is NOT a permanent magnet.

B

In most objects, these mini-magnets point in all directions, so they cancel each other out and are **not magnetic**.

Whereas, **in a permanent magnet**, all the magnetic microfields in the atoms are lined up in the same direction, which creates a bigger magnetic field.

Permanent magnet

B

B

When a magnet comes close to a metal paper clip, the paper clip becomes magnetic.

Some materials **become magnets** when a magnet is brought close to them, as their magnetic microfields align. When they're **moved away from the magnet**, their atomic mini-magnets become disordered again and **stop behaving like magnets**.

Magnetism generates electricity

Michael Faraday (1777–1851) was a British physicist who studied electromagnetism.

Based on Ørsted's experiment, Faraday thought that if an electric current creates a magnetic field, then perhaps the opposite could also happen—in other words, magnetism could create electricity.

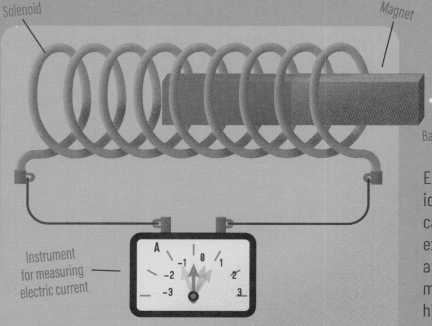

Solenoid

Magnet

Back and forth movement of the magnet

Instrument for measuring electric current

A

Encouraged by this idea, in 1830 he carried out a simple experiment using a solenoid and a magnet that led him to make a great discovery.

When the magnet got close to the solenoid, an electric current appeared.

When the magnet moved away, a current also appeared but in the opposite direction.

As soon as the magnet stopped moving, the current disappeared.

If we leave the magnet still and we move the solenoid away from or toward the magnet, the same thing happens: an electric current appears in the circuit. It doesn't matter what we move, the solenoid, the magnet, or both; the important thing is that they are moving in relation to the other.

THE FASTER THE MOVEMENT, THE GREATER THE CURRENT.

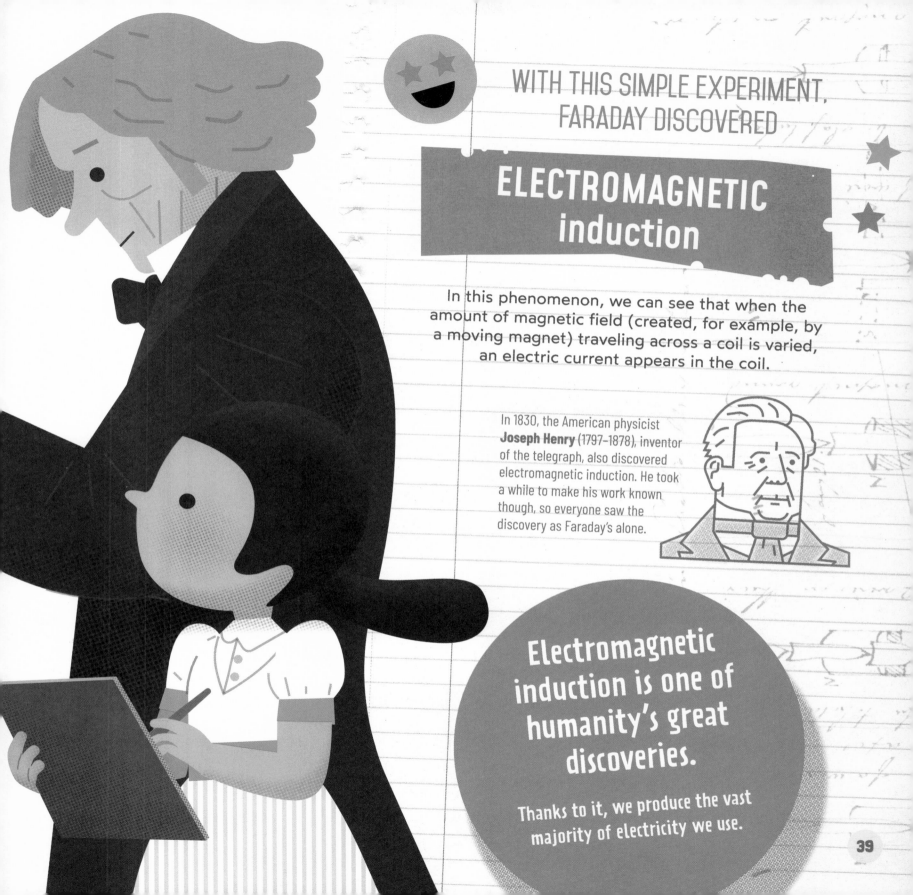

WITH THIS SIMPLE EXPERIMENT, FARADAY DISCOVERED

ELECTROMAGNETIC induction

In this phenomenon, we can see that when the amount of magnetic field (created, for example, by a moving magnet) traveling across a coil is varied, an electric current appears in the coil.

In 1830, the American physicist **Joseph Henry** (1797–1878), inventor of the telegraph, also discovered electromagnetic induction. He took a while to make his work known though, so everyone saw the discovery as Faraday's alone.

Electromagnetic induction is one of humanity's great discoveries.

Thanks to it, we produce the vast majority of electricity we use.

PRODUCING ELECTRICITY

Nowadays, we use electricity for nearly everything. Since we discovered how to generate it around 250 years ago, demand for it has risen continuously.

We produce electricity to cover most of our energy needs mainly using the electromagnetic induction discovered by Faraday.

Electric generator

This is a device that converts circular movement (mechanical energy) into electricity (electrical energy) through electromagnetic induction.

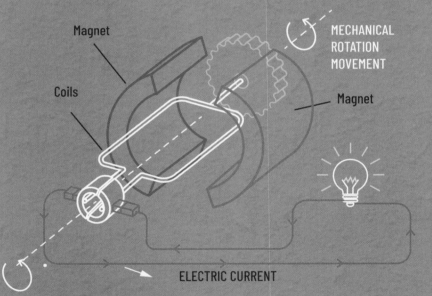

Magnet

Coils

MECHANICAL ROTATION MOVEMENT

Magnet

ELECTRIC CURRENT

In a similar way to Faraday's experiment, if we spin some conductor coils in a magnetic field created by a magnet, this produces an electric current. Remember, it doesn't matter if we rotate the spirals or the magnet, the result will be the same. The important thing is that they are moving in relation to one another.

BLADE

GENERATOR

WIND TURBINES use wind to move their blades and make the generator work.

HYDROELECTRIC power stations use the movement of water to rotate the **TURBINES**.

WATER

TURBINE

DAM

There are lots of types of electric power stations that use different kinds of energy to turn the turbines. But essentially, they all do the same thing: make coils spin round in a magnetic field to generate electricity.

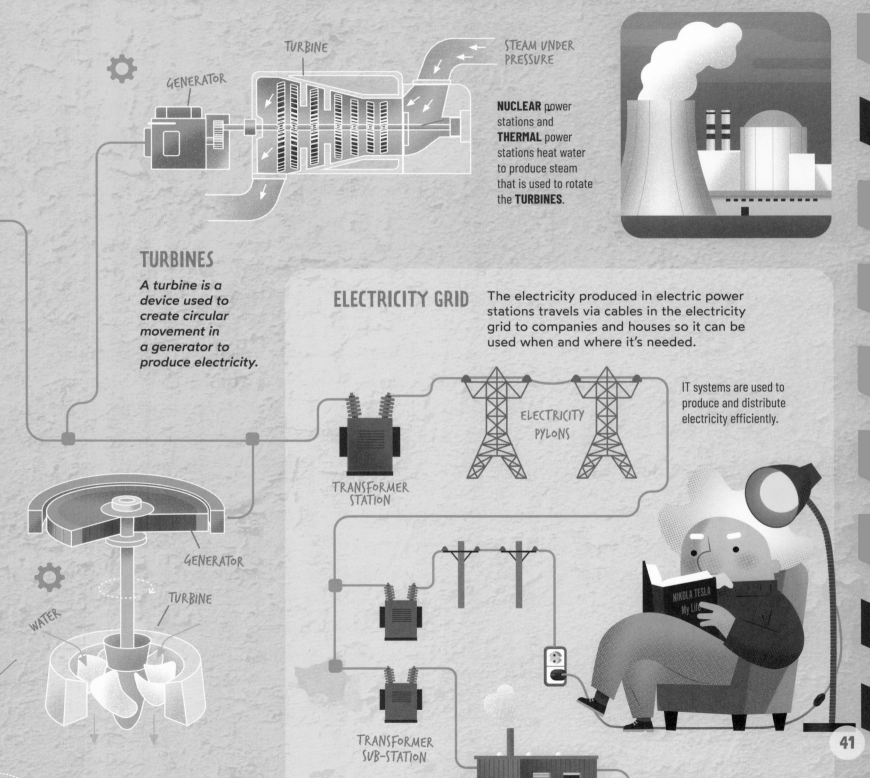

GENERATOR

TURBINE

STEAM UNDER PRESSURE

NUCLEAR power stations and **THERMAL** power stations heat water to produce steam that is used to rotate the **TURBINES**.

TURBINES

A turbine is a device used to create circular movement in a generator to produce electricity.

ELECTRICITY GRID

The electricity produced in electric power stations travels via cables in the electricity grid to companies and houses so it can be used when and where it's needed.

IT systems are used to produce and distribute electricity efficiently.

ELECTRICITY PYLONS

TRANSFORMER STATION

GENERATOR

TURBINE

WATER

NIKOLA TESLA My Life

TRANSFORMER SUB-STATION

THE FIELD

One of the problems that the nineteenth century physicists had was to explain forces that acted at a distance. How come an electric charge attracted or repelled another without touching it? And how could a magnet move pieces of iron at a distance?

To explain how these things acted at a distance, Faraday had a brilliant idea: he imagined that the forces an electric charge exerted on another, or a magnet on another magnet, could be represented by lines of force or field lines that form what we call the FIELD.

A magnet creates a magnetic field $\vec{B}$.

This magnetic field is responsible for the forces of attraction felt by other magnetic objects nearby.

Here, the field is less intense.

Here, the field has little effect.

Here, the field is more intense.

The electric charges create an electric field $\vec{E}$.

When a charge finds itself in an electric field, it feels a force that could be attraction or repulsion.

When two electric charges have the same sign, they repel one another.

When two electric charges have a different sign, they are attracted.

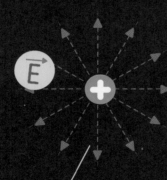

We show the electric field using force lines in a radial pattern.

In positive charges, the field lines leave.

In negative charges, the field lines enter.

A field is the region of space where electric charges and magnets exert their effect.

When Faraday put forward his idea of a field, it was not very popular with scientists at the time (despite being one of the most important ideas in modern physics).

Faraday came from a poor background and he didn't have a good education in mathematics. Because of this, he was unable to develop one of his greatest ideas: a theory unifying electricity and magnetism.

It was James Clerk Maxwell (1831–1879) who carried out this task.

Maxwell was a brilliant Scottish physicist and mathematician who took Faraday's ideas very seriously. Thanks to his excellent knowledge of mathematics, he was able to write his four famous equations that describe all electric and magnetic phenomenon, including everything we have seen about electric charges and magnets, and the experiments done by Ørsted and Faraday.

These equations are based on the *idea of fields* and *bring together* electricity and magnetism *in a single branch of physics*:

ELECTROMAGNETISM

The magic of Maxwell's laws is that they explain ALL electromagnetic phenomenon using the electric field $\vec{E}$ and the magnetic field $\vec{B}$.

ELECTROMAG

When Maxwell used his equations, he got a surprise: he worked out from them that there were waves of electricity and magnetism, in other words, electromagnetic waves.

WHAT IS A WAVE?

It is a disturbance that travels through space and carries energy but does NOT carry matter.

For example, when we throw a pebble into a pond, the disturbance caused by the impact produces concentric waves that travel in the water.

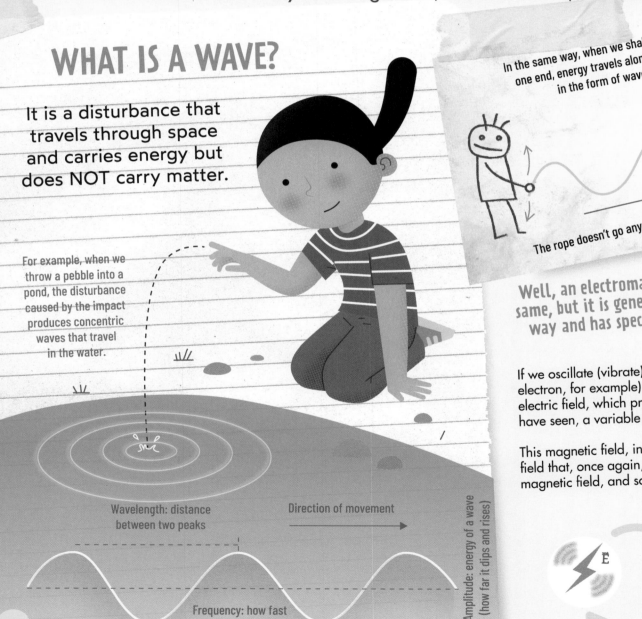

In the same way, when we shake a rope at one end, energy travels along the rope in the form of waves.

The rope doesn't go anywhere. Only energy does.

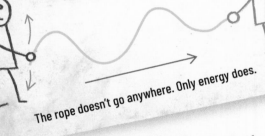

Well, an electromagnetic wave is the same, but it is generated in a different way and has special characteristics.

If we oscillate (vibrate) an electric charge (an electron, for example), we create a variable electric field, which produces, exactly as we have seen, a variable magnetic field.

This magnetic field, in turn, creates an electric field that, once again, produces another magnetic field, and so on.

Wavelength: distance between two peaks

Direction of movement

Amplitude: energy of a wave (how far it dips and rises)

Frequency: how fast a wave oscillates (number of waves per second)

NETIC WAVES

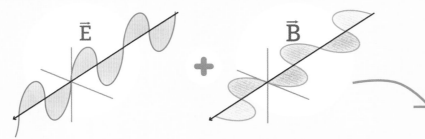
$\vec{E}$ + $\vec{B}$

This is how we get a variable electromagnetic field, in other words, an electric field **E** and a magnetic field **B** combined, which oscillate and generate further electric and magnetic fields by traveling through space, carrying energy from one place to another.

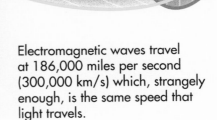

Electromagnetic waves travel at 186,000 miles per second (300,000 km/s) which, strangely enough, is the same speed that light travels.

Maxwell thought this was too much of a coincidence, so he concluded that light must be a kind of electromagnetic wave too.

LIGHT IS AN ELECTROMAGNETIC WAVE

A puzzle that had always intrigued humanity had finally been solved: WHAT IS LIGHT?

Well, visible light is the small part of the electromagnetic waves that we can see with our eyes.

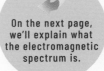

On the next page, we'll explain what the electromagnetic spectrum is.

The electromagnetic spectrum

The electromagnetic spectrum is all electromagnetic waves put together, arranged by wavelength.

If the waves are traveling at the same speed, the shorter a wave is, the faster it oscillates (the higher its frequency) and the more energy it has. And the longer a wave is, the slower it oscillates (the lower its frequency) and the less energy it has.

It's not the same sailing in a calm sea with few waves (low frequency) as in a rough sea with lots of waves (high frequency).

It's the same with electromagnetic waves: some don't oscillate much and are really long, like radio waves, while others are very short and oscillate super fast, like gamma rays.

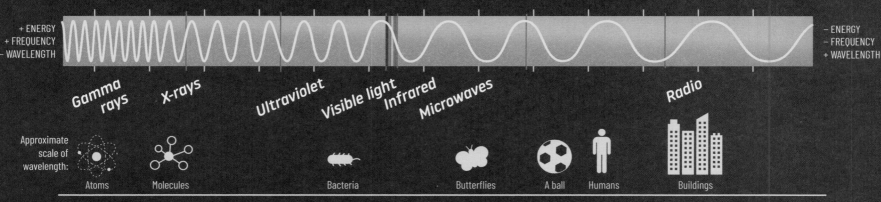

+ ENERGY
+ FREQUENCY
– WAVELENGTH

– ENERGY
– FREQUENCY
+ WAVELENGTH

Gamma rays · X-rays · Ultraviolet · Visible light · Infrared · Microwaves · Radio

Approximate scale of wavelength:

Atoms · Molecules · Bacteria · Butterflies · A ball · Humans · Buildings

A lot of the technology used by humans is based on machines capable of giving out or receiving electromagnetic waves.

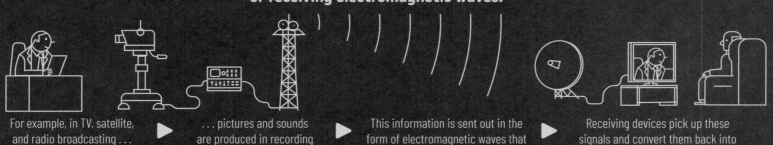

For example, in TV, satellite, and radio broadcasting . . .

. . . pictures and sounds are produced in recording studios.

This information is sent out in the form of electromagnetic waves that travel through space.

Receiving devices pick up these signals and convert them back into sounds and pictures.

We also use electromagnetic waves to heat food in microwaves, to receive data and communicate with cell phones, to know where we are with global positioning systems (GPS), to produce X-rays, in remote controls that use infrared, and lots more.

We are electromagnetism

The world around us is made of atoms: water, soil, air, rocks, metals, books, animals (including ourselves), plants . . . in short: EVERYTHING. And this means that everything is made of electrically charged particles that interact.

When we touch something (anything—a ball, an animal, water), in fact what we feel is the repulsive (repelling) force between the electrons in its atoms and our own.

Strictly speaking, we never really touch anything.

Although we draw an atom like this to make it easier to understand, the nucleus and the electrons are much smaller in size and the distance between them is much greater.

In fact, most of the atom is empty and it is electromagnetic interactions that keep the electrons around the nucleus.

Think about it: you can stroke your pet thanks to electromagnetism, but you aren't really touching it.

Most of the atom is empty!

which means . . .

Most of everything (including ourselves) is hollow!

IMAGINE IF ELECTROMAGNETISM DIDN'T EXIST

Without the electric force of repulsion between electrons in atoms, we could walk through walls or sink into the ground, as no force would hold us back.

Well, okay, if it weren't for electromagnetism, there would be no atoms and the Universe would be very different from the one we know.

ALSO AVAILABLE

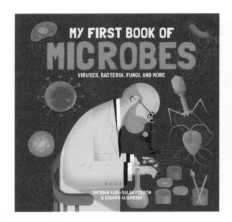
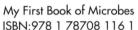

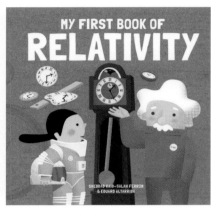

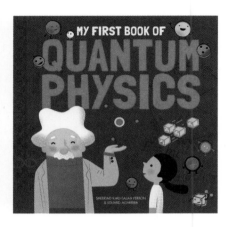

My First Book of Microbes
ISBN:978 1 78708 116 1

My First Book of Relativity
ISBN:978 1 78708 033 1

My First Book of Quantum Physics
ISBN:978 1 78708 010 2

ACKNOWLEDGMENTS

Sheddad—To my two main physicists, **Diego Jurado** and **Carles Muñoz**, for proofreading the book.
To **Júlia Jurado Alemany**, for her vision and for helping me to see what I couldn't see.
To **Mariona Esquerda Ciutat**, for her comments and her brilliant, educational videos on her channel La Dimoni de Maxwell.
To **Helena**, for proofreading and correcting the text and for always being there. And, of course, to **Inma**, **Tarek**, and **Unai**. I love you.

Eduard—A thousand thanks from me to all the people who have made this book possible, especially **Meli** but also **Pere**, **Lourdes**, and **Ariadna** for their constant support and infinite patience.
Also to my beta-readers, **Xavi Villanueva** and **Picu Oms**, who have been generous enough to see what we could no longer see.
To **Andrea Reece** for the translation into English.

And to Michael Faraday, Thales of Miletus, Benjamin Franklin, James Clerk Maxwell . . . and to all the scientists, both men and women, whose work has made, is making, and will continue to make it possible to go further and further.

FSC
www.fsc.org
MIX
Paper | Supporting responsible forestry
FSC® C020056